To Maurice Richardson,
If you think it, so
Shall it be.

Linda Sauget

If You Think It

LINDA SAUGET

BALBOA.
PRESS
A DIVISION OF HAY HOUSE

Balboa Press books may be ordered through booksellers or by contacting:

Balboa Press
A Division of Hay House
1663 Liberty Drive
Bloomington, IN 47403
www.balboapress.com
1-(877) 407-4847

ISBN: 978-1-4525-3933-1 (sc)
ISBN: 978-1-4525-3932-4 (hc)
ISBN: 978-1-4525-3931-7 (e)

Library of Congress Control Number: 2011916293

Printed in the United States of America

Balboa Press rev. date: 9/26/2011

To my son, Matthew, whose name means "gift from God," and who has always been that to me

We are what we think.
All that we are arises
With our thoughts.
With our thoughts,
We make our world.

—Buddha

Contents

List of Illustrations

Preface

Is there a saying you keep in your wallet, on your refrigerator, or at your desk that inspires you? Do you have a favorite motto or philosophy that encourages and uplifts you?

If You Think It features a collection of timeless and timely quotations on a subject all great philosophers agree on. The single most important determinant in creating a quality life, achieving success in any endeavor, and living the life of your dreams, is simply this: each thought has the power to impact your life positively or negatively and at every moment you decide.

Thoughts are tangible things. As Wayne Dyer says, "If you change the way you look at things, the things you look at change." The direction of your life moves in the direction of your thoughts.

Remind yourself about the power of your thoughts by reading a quotation each day or by randomly turning to a message. With your thoughts you create your world.

Acknowledgments

Gratitude comes easily to me, and I go through every day in awe of all there is to be grateful for. So many people have been pivotal in supporting, encouraging, and mentoring me that it is my honor to say thank you.

First, to Matt, who provided me with the test-tube case of the power of thought. In a way, this book was in the works since your birth. I could not be prouder.

To my brother and hero, Phillip, you have always inspired me. You did not have to learn this teaching; you *are* this teaching.

To my dear friends, how blessed I am to be surrounded by your love and support. Thank you, Eric and Debbie Jacobson, Jim and Grace Barber, Hervey Ross, Lynda Hammond, Val Jennings, Steve Bradbery, Enrique Camacho, Terry Conover, Shantelle Moxie, Carolina Small, Suchita Kaundin, Nohemy and Freddie Contreras, Bonnie and Eric Ross, Bob and Kathy Freytag, Bob Stevens, Tony Deliso, Frank Rhoads, Steve Leibovitz, and AZ Zimmerman. Your insight, faith and encouragement have meant so much to me. Thank you.

To the extraordinary team at Balboa Press—thank you for your insights, guidance and support.

And finally, to my parents, who have passed on but are with me every day. There are no better examples of optimism, positive attitude, loyalty, and love.

Chapter I
Thought

We all have a predominant outlook on life, a way of seeing things. What we create, who we are, and what we do are all expressions of thought. Our expectations, our views of the world, our attitudes, our behaviors, and our personalities all come from our thoughts.

Some people think our worldview develops as a result of the experiences we've had. We are optimistic or pessimistic, lucky or unlucky, successful or unsuccessful all because of the things that have happened to us. We have accumulated the evidence of this.

In reality, the reverse is true: all of the "evidence" is the result of our thoughts. Our thoughts come first whether we realize it or not. It is no wonder that Peace Pilgrim said, "If you realized how powerful your thoughts are, you would never think a negative thought."

Two people can view the exact same event but have a different interpretation of what they see. Two people from the same family can recall a family situation but remember the experience differently. That's because the outlook we bring informs our memory. The thoughts we have help focus what we notice. We always gather the evidence to make ourselves right and to prove our point of view.

If I have the thought that the people I work with are unfriendly, I am going to notice evidence of that. Someone who is preoccupied and walks by me without really noticing me is going to provide proof to me that I work with unfriendly people. If I have the thought that I work with friendly people, I may be the first one to say hello and smile at the person walking by, or this may not even register in my mind as an unfriendly gesture. I may recognize that the person is preoccupied, or I may not even have the thought that I was snubbed. Nothing negative registers as the person walks by.

It may sound simplistic, but what we notice and what we don't notice are related to how we think. The actions that we take depend upon what we think, and our attitudes are the results of our thoughts. Our world is a reflection of our thoughts.

Albert Einstein once said the most important decision we will ever make is deciding whether we live in a hostile universe or a friendly universe, because that decision will color everything in our lives. We make the decision; we have the thought. Then all of the evidence supports that point of view.

Perception follows our thoughts; our interpretations follow our thoughts. What we think creates our world.

The ancestor of every action is a thought.

Ralph Waldo Emerson, American poet and essayist

1803-1882

Great men are they who see that the spiritual is stronger than any material force, that thoughts rule the world.

Ralph Waldo Emerson, American poet and essayist

1803-1882

The world is a product of thought. It is a creation of the mind.

Swami Muktananda, Indian Hindu guru, founder of Siddha Yoga

1908-1982

We create our own world by our own thoughts. And thus we make our own heaven, and our own hell.

Swami Muktananda, Indian Hindu guru, founder of Siddha Yoga

1908-1982

As he thinketh in his heart, so is he.

Proverbs 23:7 KJV

If you are distressed by anything external, the pain is not due to the thing itself but to your own estimate of it; and this you have the power to revoke at any moment.

Marcus Aurelius, Roman Emperor

AD 121-180

**It is the mind that maketh good or ill,
that maketh wretch or happy, rich or poor.**

Edmund Spenser, English poet

1552-1599

I think, therefore I am.

Rene Descartes, French philosopher, mathematician, scientist

1596-1650

All that is comes from the mind; it is based on the mind, it is fashioned by the mind.

The Pali Canon, sacred literature of Buddhism

First century BC

You are today where your thoughts have brought you. You will be tomorrow where your thoughts take you.

James Allen, British philosopher, poet, inspirational writer

1864-1912

**Men are not influenced by things,
but by their thoughts about things.**

Epictetus, Greek philosopher

c. AD 50-c. AD 138

The highest possible stage in moral culture is when we recognize that we ought to control our thoughts.

Charles Darwin, English naturalist

1809-1882

Mind is the master power that molds and makes, and we are mind, and evermore we take the tool of thought, and stating what we will, bring forth a thousand joys, a thousand ills.

James Allen, British philosopher, poet, inspirational writer

1864-1912

Your life is an expression of all your thoughts.

Marcus Aurelius, Roman emperor

121-180

A man is what he thinks about all day long.

Ralph Waldo Emerson, American poet and essayist

1803-1882

A man is literally what he thinks.

James Allen, British philosopher, poet, inspirational writer

1864-1912

You cannot escape the results of your thoughts . . . Whatever your present environment may be, you will fall, remain or rise with your thoughts, your vision, your ideal.

James Allen, British philosopher, poet, inspirational writer

1864-1912

Thought makes the whole dignity of man; therefore endeavor to think well, that is the only morality.

Blaise Pascal, French scientist and religious philosopher

1623-1662

The more man meditates upon good thoughts, the better will be his world and the world at large.

Confucius, Chinese philosopher

c. 551 BC-479 BC

Good thoughts and actions can never produce bad results; bad thoughts and actions can never produce good results.

James Allen, British philosopher, poet, inspirational writer

1864-1912

All that a man does outwardly is but the expression and completion of his inward thought. To work effectively, he must think clearly; to act nobly, he must think nobly.

William Ellery Channing, American Unitarian preacher

1780-1842

There is nothing either good or bad, but thinking makes it so.

William Shakespeare, English dramatist and poet

1564-1616

There is the positive side and the negative side and at every moment I decide.

William James, American psychologist and philosopher

1842-1910

Every life has its dark and cheerful hours. Happiness comes from choosing which to remember.

Anonymous

**We choose our joys and sorrow long
before we experience them.**

Kahlil Gibran, Lebanese-American poet and novelist

1883-1931

**We awaken in others the same attitude of mind we hold
toward them.**

Elbert Hubbard, American writer, publisher, artist, philosopher

1856-1915

Very little is needed to make a happy life; it is all within yourself, in your way of thinking.

Marcus Aurelius, Roman emperor

121-180

We think in secret, and it comes to pass—our world is but our looking glass.

James Allen, British philosopher, poet, inspirational writer

1864-1912

In a universe where "like goes to like," and "birds of a feather flock together," we attract to us what we emanate.[1]

David R. Hawkins, MD, PhD, American psychiatrist, lecturer, writer

1927-

[1] David R. Hawkins, MD, PhD, *Power vs. Force: The Hidden Determinants of Human Behavior.* Carlsbad, Calif.: Hay House, 2002, 129.

Thoughts become things! This is the underlying principle that turns a wish into reality. It's what powers positive thinking and gives rise to the Law of Attraction, and it's why visualizations work.[2]

Mike Dooley, American writer, motivational speaker

1961-

---

[2] Mike Dooley, *Infinite Possibilities*. New York: Atria Books, 2009, 7.

Remember that life is very simple. You create your experiences by your thinking and feeling patterns.[3]

Louise L. Hay, American motivational writer, publisher

1926-

[3] Louise L. Hay, *Everyday Positive Thinking*. Carlsbad, Calif.: Hay House, 2004, 444.

Nothing can occur in your life experience without your invitation of it through your thought.[4]

Esther Hicks, American inspirational speaker and author

1948-

---

[4]   Esther and Jerry Hicks, *Ask and It Is Given*. Carlsbad, Calif.: Hay House, 2005, 27.

Thoughts of a kind have a natural affinity. While the negative thinker tends to draw back to himself negative results, the positive thinker activates the world around him positively.[5]

Norman Vincent Peale, American Protestant preacher and author

1898-1993

[5] Norman Vincent Peale, *Positive Thinking Every Day*. New York: Fireside Press, 1993, 13.

The game of life is the game of boomerangs. Our thoughts, deeds and words return to us sooner or later, with astounding accuracy.[6]

Florence Scovel Shinn, American artist, illustrator, author

1871-1940

---

[6] Florence Scovel Shinn, *The Game of Life and How to Play It*. New York: The Penguin Group, 1925, 39.

Thought is cause; experience is effect. If you don't like the effects in your life, you have to change the nature of your thinking.[7]

Marianne Williamson, American spiritual teacher, author, lecturer

1952-

[7] Marianne Williamson, *A Return to Love: Reflections on the Principles of A Course in Miracles*. New York: Harper Collins Publishers, Inc., 1992, 24.

Thought creates all experience.[8]

Richard Carlson, American author, psychologist, motivational speaker

1961-2006

---

[8] Richard Carlson and Joseph Bailey, *Slowing Down to the Speed of Life*. New York: HarperOne, 1997, 27.

Thought is the power that creates human experience—the ultimate force that creates, shapes, and transforms our lives.[9]

Richard Carlson, American author, psychologist, motivational speaker

1961-2006

---

[9]   Richard Carlson and Joseph Bailey, *Slowing Down to the Speed of Life*. New York: HarperOne, 1997, 22.

You are what you think.[10]

Napoleon Hill and W. Clement Stone

Napoleon Hill 1883-1970, American author, journalist, lecturer.

W. Clement Stone 1902-2002, American businessman, philanthropist, self-help author.

[10] Napoleon Hill and W. Clement Stone, *Success Through a Positive Mental Attitude.* New York: Pocket Books, 1960, 40.

Everyone is a mirror image of yourself—your own thinking coming back at you.[11]

Byron Katie, American author, speaker

1942-

---

[11]   Byron Katie, *Loving What Is*. New York: Three Rivers Press, 2002, 27.

Back of everything is the immutable law of the Universe—that what you are is but the effect. Your thoughts are the cause.[12]

Robert Collier, American self-help author

1885-1950

---

[12] Robert Collier, *The Secret of the Ages.* New York: The Penguin Group, 2007, 160.

It isn't life's events, but how one reacts to them and the attitude that one has about them, that determines whether such events have a positive or negative effect on one's life, whether they're experienced as opportunity or as stress.[13]

David R. Hawkins, MD, PhD,
American psychiatrist, lecturer, writer

1927-

[13] David R. Hawkins, MD, PhD, *Power vs. Force: The Hidden Determinants of Human Behavior.* Carlsbad, Calif.: Hay House, 2002, 72.

Happiness is wholly independent of position, wealth, or
material possession. It is a state of mind which we ourselves
have the power to control—and that
control lies with our thinking.[14]

Claude M. Bristol, American journalist, author

1891-1951

---

[14] Claude M. Bristol, *The Magic of Believing.* New York: Pocket
Books, 1948, 178.

Whatever we think about and thank about we bring about.[15]

John Demartini, DC, American author, teacher

1954-

---

[15] John Demartini, DC, quoted by Rhonda Byrne, *The Secret*. New York: Atria Books, 2006, 75.

There is a deep tendency in human nature for us to become precisely what we habitually imagine ourselves as being.[16]

Norman Vincent Peale, American Protestant preacher and author

1898-1993

---

[16] Norman Vincent Peale, *Positive Thinking for a Time Like This*, Englewood Cliffs, NJ: Prentice-Hall, Inc., 1975, 87.

Your life today is the result of your thinking yesterday. Your life tomorrow will be determined by what you think today.[17]

John C. Maxwell, Evangelical Christian pastor, author, and speaker

1947-

---

[17] John C. Maxwell, *Think on These Things: Meditations for Leaders.* Kansas City: Beacon Hill Press, 1999, 13.

The thoughts we think, the words we speak, the beliefs we accept, shape our tomorrows.[18]

Louise L. Hay, American motivational writer, publisher

1926-

---

[18]   Louise L. Hay, *Life!*, Carlsbad, Calif.: Hay House, 1995, 91.

The world in which you live is not primarily determined by outward conditions and circumstances but by the thoughts that habitually occupy your mind.[19]

Norman Vincent Peale, American Protestant preacher and author

1898-1993

---

[19] Norman Vincent Peale, *The Power of Positive Thinking: 10 Traits for Maximum Results.* New York: Fireside Press, 2003, 169.

Happiness is not a possession to be prized; it is a quality of thought, a state of mind.[20]

Daphne Du Maurier, English author and playwright

1907-1989

---

[20] Daphne Du Maurier, *Rebecca*, New York: HarperCollins, 1997, 6.

Perhaps the biggest gift that humankind has been given is the choice to decide what thoughts and attitudes we put in our minds.[21]

Gerald G. Jampolsky and Diane V. Cirincione

Co-founders of the Center for Attitudinal Healing, Tiburon, California

Gerald G. Jampolsky 1925-

Diane V. Cirincione 1946-

---

[21] Gerald G. Jampolsky and Diane V. Cirincione, *Change Your Mind, Change Your Life*. New York: Bantam Books, 1993, 4.

We lift ourselves by our thought . . . . If you want to enlarge your life, you must first enlarge your thought of it and of yourself.[22]

Orison Swett Marden, American writer

1850-1924

---

[22] Orison Swett Marden, *You Can, But Will You?* New York: Thomas Y Crowell Publishers, 1920, 100.

Nothing has any power over me other than that which I give it through my conscious thoughts.[23]

Anthony Robbins, American self-help author and success coach

1960-

---

[23] Anthony Robbins, *Unlimited Power.* New York: Free Press, 1986, 85.

**You control your future, your destiny.
What you think about comes about.**[24]

Mark Victor Hansen, American author and motivational speaker

1948-

---

[24] Mark Victor Hansen, Barbara Nichols and Patty Hansen, *Out of the Blue: Delight Comes into Our Lives*. New York: Cliff Street Books, 1997, 91.

There is power in our thoughts. We create our own surroundings by the thoughts we think.[25]

Betty J. Eadie, American author

1948-

[25] Betty J. Eadie, *Embraced By the Light*, New York: Bantam Books, 1994, 58

The Law of Attraction attracts to you everything you need, according to the nature of your thought life. Thought rules the world.[26]

Joseph Murphy, Divine Science minister and author

1898-1981

---

[26] Joseph Murphy, *Your Infinite Power to Be Rich.* Englewood, NJ: Prentice Hall, 1966, 29.

Chapter II

Belief

Our attitudes, dreams, actions, and accomplishments reflect our beliefs. Underneath everything we do and everything we think, there is a belief. While doubt closes doors, belief opens them. We shape our life according to our beliefs. Everything grows out of our beliefs, even if we are not conscious of it.

Albert Einstein said it is better to believe than to disbelieve, for in believing, everything is brought into the realm of possibility. If we can live in possibility, then everything is possible. There is hope. There is an opening. If we live in the belief that something is impossible, then it will be impossible. In the realm of impossibility, there is no need to try. There is no need to take action. There is no hope. If I have a belief that I cannot do something, that becomes a self-fulfilling prophecy. But the opposite holds true too. If I have a belief that I can do something, it lives in the realm of possibility, and I will move toward it.

Whatever beliefs we have are true for us. We will see evidence to support our beliefs, because we will filter and notice the things that we believe to be true. That is why two people can witness the same thing but have a different interpretation. We "see" according to our beliefs.

If we can choose to be positive or negative, and a positive or negative consequence flows from that, why not choose to be positive? If we can believe in possibility or impossibility, why not choose to live in possibility?

The direction of our lives follows our beliefs. The result of any endeavor follows our beliefs. Our opinions follow our beliefs. First comes the belief, and the rest necessarily follows. Put on rose-colored glasses, and roses will bloom. Put on glasses of "no, it will never happen," and you will be 100 percent right. What we believe is what is so for us.

Believe that you have it, and you have it.

Latin proverb

Man is what he believes.

Anton Chekhov, Russian playwright, short story writer

1860-1904

To accomplish great things, we must not only act, but also dream; not only plan but also believe.

Anatole France, French poet, journalist, novelist

1844-1924

Whatsoever ye shall ask in prayer, believing, ye shall receive.

Matthew 21:22 KJV

**Whether you think you can or whether you think you can't—
you are right.**

Henry Ford, American industrialist, automobile manufacturer

1863-1947

Believe that life is worth living and your belief will help create the fact.

William James, American psychologist and philosopher

1842-1910

What things soever ye desire, when ye pray, believe that ye receive them, and ye shall have them.

Mark 11:24 KJV

Faith is to believe what we do not see and the reward of faith is to see what we believe.

St. Augustine, Latin philosopher and theologian

350-430

Men are disturbed not by things but by the views they take of them.

Epictetus, Greek philosopher

c. AD 50-c. AD 138

No man is unhappy unless he believes he is.

Publilus Syrus, Latin writer of maxims

First century BC

Walk by faith, not by sight.

2 Corinthians 5:7 KJV

Faith consists in believing when it is beyond the power of reason to believe. It is not enough that a thing be possible for it to be believed.

Voltaire, French philosopher and author

1694-1778

If thou canst believe, all things are possible to him that believeth.

Mark 9:23 KJV

They conquer who believe they can.

Ralph Waldo Emerson, American poet and essayist

1803-1882

It is done unto you as you believe.

Jesus Christ

Nurture your mind with great thoughts. To believe in the heroic makes heroes.

Benjamin Disraeli, British prime minister

1804-1881

It is by believing in roses that one brings them to bloom.

French proverb

To believe a thing is impossible is to make it so.

French proverb

Man is made by his belief. As he believes, so he is.

Bhagavad Gita,

Indian religious text

**If I keep a green bough in my heart,
the singing bird will come.**

Chinese proverb

A person who doubts himself is like a man who would enlist in the ranks of his enemies and bear arms against himself.

Alexander Dumas, French novelist

1802-1870

**If you think you can win, you can win.
Faith is necessary to victory.**

William Hazlitt, English essayist

1778-1830

Everything depends on one's opinion. We suffer according to our opinion. One is as miserable or as happy as one believes oneself to be.

Seneca, Roman philosopher

c. 3 BC-65 AD

Achieving starts with believing.

Anonymous

Our beliefs about ourselves are the most telling factors in determining our level of success and happiness in life.[27]

Wayne Dyer, American self-help author, speaker

1940-

---

[27] Wayne Dyer, *Staying on the Path*, Carlsbad, Calif.: Hay House, 2004, 135.

Believe it and you'll see it. Know it and you'll *be* it![28]

Wayne Dyer, American self-help author, speaker

1940-

---

[28] Ibid., 170.

What we *believe* about anything will determine our attitudes about it, create our feelings, direct our action, and in each instance, help us to do well or poorly, succeed or fail.[29]

Shad Helmstetter, PhD, American author and lecturer

1943-

---

[29]   Shad Helmstetter, PhD, *What to Say When You Talk to Your Self.* New York: Pocket Books, 1982, 68.

No matter what we are told or who says it, if we believe it, then through our mystic manifesting powers we, as generators behind the thought, empower the thought to create itself in a material form or circumstance.[30]

Terry Cole-Whittaker, New Thought minister, author, lecturer

1940-

---

[30] Terry Cole-Whittaker, *Live Your Bliss*. Novato, Calif.: New World Library, 2009, 8.

**Belief is the thermostat that regulates
what we accomplish in life.**[31]

David J. Schwartz, PhD, American professor, author, speaker

1927-

---

[31] David J. Schwartz, PhD, *The Magic of Thinking BIG*. New York: Fireside Press, 2007, 14.

The deepest ocean—the tallest mountain, the most powerful animal cannot believe. Only man can believe. The height of man's success is determined by the depth of his belief.[32]

Zig Ziglar, motivational speaker, author

1926-

---

[32] Zig Ziglar, *See You at the Top*. Gretna, Louisiana: Pelican Publishing Company, 1982, 387.

Whatever you believe with feeling becomes reality.[33]

Brian Tracey, Canadian self-help author

1944-

---

[33] Brian Tracey, *Maximum Achievement: Strategies and Skills that Will Unlock Your Hidden Powers to Succeed.* New York: Simon & Schuster, 1993, 45.

Mind is all that counts. You can be whatever you make up your mind to be.[34]

Robert Collier, American self-help author

1885-1950

---

[34] Robert Collier, *Secret of the Ages: The Master Code to Abundance and Achievement.* New York: Penguin Group USA/JP Tarcher, 1925, 3.

What we can or cannot do, what we consider possible or impossible, is rarely a function of our true capability. It is more likely a function of our beliefs about who we are.[35]

Anthony Robbins, American self-help author and success coach

1960-

---

[35] Anthony Robbins, *Awaken the Giant Within.* New York: Summit Books, 1991, 413.

So many of our dreams at first seem impossible, then they seem improbable, and then, when we summon the will, they soon become inevitable.[36]

Christopher Reeve, American actor, director, author

1952-2004

---

[36] Christopher Reeve, *Still Me*. New York: Random House, 1999, 302.

If you develop the absolute sense of certainty that powerful beliefs provide, then you can get yourself to accomplish virtually anything, including those things that other people are certain are impossible.[37]

Anthony Robbins, American self-help author and success coach

1960-

---

[37]   Robbins, 1991, 82.

Believe it is possible to solve your problems. Tremendous things happen to the believer. So believe the answer will come. It will.[38]

Norman Vincent Peale, American Protestant preacher and author

1898-1993

---

[38] Norman Vincent Peale, *You Can If You Think You Can*. New York: Fireside Press, 1992, 39.

Gradually I discovered that there is a golden thread that runs through all teaching and then work for those who sincerely accept and apply them, and that thread can be named in a single word—belief.[39]

Claude M. Bristol, American journalist, author

1891-1951

---

[39] Claude M. Bristol, *The Magic of Believing.* New York: Pocket Books, 1948, 5

Believe Big. The size of your success is determined by the size of your belief.[40]

David J. Schwartz, American professor, author, speaker

1927-

---

[40] David J. Schwartz, PhD, *The Magic of Thinking BIG.* New York: Simon & Schuster, 1987, 21.

Your belief determines your action and your action determines your results, but first you have to believe.[41]

Mark Victor Hansen, American author and motivational speaker

1948-

---

[41] Mark Victor Hansen, *Dare to Win*. New York: Berkley Books, 1994, 102.

Chapter III

Manifestation

Everything we create and everything we achieve comes from the mind. Whether it is the shape our life has taken, the work we do for a living, or the relationships we have, everything we have achieved is the result of our thoughts. We are the creator of our world, whether we are aware of it or not. As we become conscious of our power, then we can shift from observing our achievements and contributions as if they were things that have happened in our life to knowing they unfold through conscious design.

Manifestation is not mysterious or magical. Rather, there is a correlation between what we focus on, what we think about, what actions we take, and the results we manifest. It is really as simple as that.

For years, I have collected quotations that were inspiring and meaningful to me. In the course of doing that, I noticed how quotations about the power of thought ran through every genre, every culture, every philosophy, and every religion from ancient times forward. I started segregating those quotations from others I had collected and had the idea of publishing them as a collection. It became something I visualized and thought about. The messages empowered me, and I believed they would empower others.

The publication of this book is an example of this philosophy: what we think about comes about. Not by magic. Not mysteriously. The manifestation of this book is the result of my vision to see this in print. It is what I have seen, believed, and thought about creating. I saw the end product as soon as I had the idea to create the book.

We can choose our thoughts, reactions, and attitudes. We can choose what goals we have and what actions we take to achieve them. In the myriad of priorities to focus on, what is most important? What do we choose to put our attention on? It does not come from outside us; the choice is uniquely ours.

The manifestation of whatever it is we desire starts in the mind with our thoughts and beliefs.

All that you achieve and all that you fail to achieve is the direct result of your own thoughts.

James Allen, British philosopher, poet, inspirational writer

1864-1912

All that we are is the result of what we have thought.

Dhammapada

Buddhist scripture, it is one of the texts from the Theravada canon

A man's life is what his thoughts make it.

Marcus Aurelius, Roman emperor

121-180

Always bear in mind that your own resolution to success is more important than any other one thing.

Abraham Lincoln, sixteenth president of the United States

1809-1865

Determine that the thing can and shall be done, and then we shall find the way.

Abraham Lincoln, sixteenth president of the United States

1809-1865

The people who get on in the world are the people who get up and look for the circumstances they want, and, if they can't find them, make them.

George Bernard Shaw, Irish playwright

1856-1950

Once you make a decision, the universe conspires to make it happen.

Ralph Waldo Emerson, American poet and essayist

1803-1882

What we are today Comes from Our thoughts of yesterday, And our present thoughts Build our life Of tomorrow. Our life is the creation of our mind.

Buddha, spiritual teacher from ancient India

c. 563-483 BC

The Buddha means "The Enlightened One."

I have always thought the actions of men are the best interpreters of their thoughts.

John Locke, British philosopher

1632-1707

You will be what you will to be.

James Allen, British philosopher, poet, inspirational writer

1864-1912

Man's greatness lies in his thought.

Blaise Pascal, French scientist and religious philosopher

1623-1662

No great improvements in the lot of mankind are possible, until a great change takes place in the fundamental constitution of their modes of thought.

John Stuart Mill, British philosopher and economist

1806-1873

Work joyfully and peacefully, knowing that thoughts and right efforts will inevitably bring about right results.

James Allen, British philosopher, poet, inspirational writer

1864-1912

Nurture great thoughts for you cannot go higher than your thoughts.

Benjamin Disraeli, British prime minister

1804-1881

A man can do all things if he but wills them.

Leon Battista Alberti, Italian author, artist, philosopher

1404-1472

The greatest discovery of my generation is that a human being can alter his life by altering his attitude of mind.

William James, American psychologist and philosopher

1842-1910

It is our attitude at the beginning of a difficult undertaking which, more than anything else, will determine its successful outcome.

William James, American psychologist and philosopher

1842-1910

Dream lofty dreams, and as you dream, so shall you become. Your Vision is the promise of what you shall one day be; your Ideal is the prophecy of what you shall at last unveil.

James Allen, British philosopher, poet, inspirational writer

1864-1912

If one advances confidently in the direction of his dreams, and endeavors to live the life he has imagined, he will meet with a success unexpected in common hours.

Henry David Thoreau, American author, poet and philosopher

1817-1862

There is a law in psychology that if you form a picture in your mind of what you would like to be, and you keep and hold that picture there long enough, you will soon become exactly as you have been thinking.

William James, American psychologist and philosopher

1842-1910

Imagination is the beginning of creation. You imagine what you desire, you will what you imagine and at last you create what you will.

George Bernard Shaw, Irish playwright

1856-1950

Have in mind the great image and the empire will come to you.

Lao-tzu, Chinese philosopher

Sixth century BC

I dream my painting and then paint my dream.

Vincent van Gogh, Dutch post-impressionist painter

1853-1890

The mind can only proceed so far upon what it knows, and can prove. There comes a point where the mind takes a leap—call it intuition or what you will—and comes out on a higher plane of knowledge.

Albert Einstein, German-born physicist and Nobel Prize winner

1879-1955

Nothing is impossible to a willing mind.

French proverb

To expect defeat is nine-tenths of defeat itself.

Francis Marion Crawford, American novelist

1854-1909

There are no limitations to the mind except those we acknowledge. Both poverty and riches are the offspring of thought.[42]

Napoleon Hill, American author, journalist, lecturer

1883-1970

---

[42] Napoleon Hill, *Think and Grow Rich.* New York: Penguin Group, 1937, 68.

**Our futures are formed by the thoughts we hold most often.
We literally become what we think about.**[43]

Wayne Dyer, American self-help author, speaker

1940-

---

[43] Wayne Dyer, *You'll See It When You Believe It*. New York: Harper Collins Publishers, 1989, 38.

Our attitudes make us rich or poor, happy or unhappy, fulfilled or incomplete. They are the single most determining factor in every action we will ever make.[44]

Shad Helmstetter, PhD, American author and lecturer

1943-

---

[44] Shad Helmstetter, PhD, *What to Say When You Talk to Your Self.* New York: Pocket Books, 1982, 163.

Your success, or failure, in meeting problems presented by the challenges of change will be determined by your mental attitude.[45]

Napoleon Hill and W. Clement Stone

Napoleon Hill 1883-1970, American author, journalist, lecturer.

W. Clement Stone 1902-2002, American businessman, philanthropist, self-help author.

---

[45] Hill and Stone, 1960, 109.

Thoughts are powerful, for they are the seeds of future circumstances, events and things.[46]

Terry Cole-Whittaker, New Thought minister, author, lecturer

1940-

---

[46] Terry Cole-Whittaker, *Live Your Bliss*. Novato, Calif.: New World Library, 2009, 6.

The quality of your thoughts and the images you hold in your mind influence both your present moment and your future results in life.[47]

Deanna Davis, PhD, American motivational writer

1970-

---

[47] Deanna Davis, PhD, *The Law of Attraction in Action*, New York: A Perigie Book, 2008, 56.

The thoughts you are thinking and the words you are declaring at this moment are creating your future.[48]

Louise L. Hay, American motivational writer, publisher

1926-

---

[48] Louise L. Hay, *You Can Heal Your Life*. Carlsbad, Calif.: Hay House, 2004, 65.

Whatever the mind of man can conceive and believe, the mind can achieve.[49]

Napoleon Hill, American motivational writer

1883-1970

---

[49] Napoleon Hill, *Success Through a Positive Mental Attitude.* New York: Prentice-Hall, 1960, 27.

Victory always starts in the head. It's a state of mind. It then spreads with such radiance and such affirmations that destiny can do nothing but obey.[50]

Douchan Gersi, documentary filmmaker

1947-

---

[50] Douchan Gersi, *Explorer.* New York: Penguin Group, USA/J.P. Tacher, 1987, 155.

Successful men and women train their minds to think only what they want to happen in their lives.[51]

Tommy Newberry, American author and motivational speaker

1967-

---

[51] Tommy Newberry, *Success Is Not an Accident.* Madison, Ga.: Tyndale Press, 1999, 139.

The imagination is literally the workshop wherein are fashioned all plans created by man.[52]

Napoleon Hill, American motivational writer

1883-1970

---

[52] Hill, 2008, 90.

When you see a thing clearly in your mind, your creative "success mechanism" within you takes over and does the job much better than you could do it by conscious effort or willpower.[53]

Maxwell Maltz, American plastic surgeon and self-help author

1899-1975

---

[53] Maxwell Maltz, *The New Psycho-Cybernetics*. Paramus, N.J.: Prentice Hall Press, 2002, 63.

It's not what you are that holds you back, it's what you think you are not.[54]

Denis Waitley, American motivational speaker and writer

1933-

---

[54] Denis Waitley, *Seeds of Greatness: The Ten Best Kept Secrets of Total Success*. New York: Pocket Books, 1983, 52.

The more you create the vibration—the mental and emotional states—of already having something, the faster you attract it to you.[55]

Jack Canfield, American motivational speaker, author

1944-

[55] Jack Canfield, *The Success Principles.* New York: Harper Collins Publishers, 2005, 91.

Index of Authors

K

Katie, Byron 42

L

Lao-Tzu 126
Lincoln, Abraham 108, 109
Locke, John 113

M

Maltz, Maxwell 142
Marden, Orison Swett 53
Maxwell, John 48
Mill, John Stuart 116
Murphy, Joseph 57

N

Newberry, Tommy 140
Nichols, Barbara 55

P

Pali Canon 12
Pascal, Blaise 21, 115
Peale, Norman Vincent 36, 47, 50, 97

R

Reeve, Christopher 95
Robbins, Anthony 54, 94, 96

S

Schwartz, David J. 90, 99
Seneca 84
Shakespeare, William 25
Shaw, George Bernard 110, 125
Shinn, Florence Scovel 37
Spenser, Edmund 10
St. Augustine 69
Stone, W. Clement 41, 134
Swami Muktananda 6, 7
Syrus, Publilus 71

T

Thoreau, Henry David 123
Tracey, Brian 92

V

Van Gogh, Vincent 127
Voltaire 73

W

Waitley, Denis 143
Williamson, Marianne 38

Z

Ziglar, Zig 91